IMAGINE LIVING HERE

THIS PLACE IS

DRY

BY
VICKI COBB

ILLUSTRATED BY
BARBARA LAVALLEE

Walker and Company
New York

For our sons:
Theo and Josh Cobb
Chip and Mark Lavallee

**The author and artist gratefully acknowledge
the support and assistance of the following:
Sally Haines of the Mesa Convention Bureau,
Anita Turnbow of the Arizona Bureau of Tourism,
the staff of the Arizona-Sonora Desert Museum,
Susan Shaffer of the Heard Museum, Desert Jeep
Tours, and the Mesa Hilton.**

First published in the United States of America in 1989 by Walker
Publishing Company, Inc.

Published simultaneously in Canada by Thomas Allen & Son Canada,
Limited, Markham, Ontario.

The Library of Congress cataloged the cloth and reinforced editions
of this book as follows:
Cobb, Vicki.
This place is dry / by Vicki Cobb : illustrated by Barbara Lavallee.
p.   cm.—(Imagine living here)
Summary: Surveys the living conditions in Arizona's Sonora Desert for
the people and unusual animals that live there. Also describes the
engineering accomplishment of Hoover Dam.
ISBN 0-8027-6854-7 —ISBN 0-8027-6866-6 (lib. bdg.)
1. Arizona—Description and travel—1981—Juvenile literature.
2. Deserts—Arizona—Juvenile literature. 3. Sonoran Desert—
Juvenile literature. [1. Sonoran Desert. 2. Deserts. 3. Arizona—
Description and travel.] I. Lavallee, Barbara, ill. II. Title.
III. Series: Cobb, Vicki. Imagine living here.
F815.C63   1989
979.1—dc19
88-25920
CIP
AC

ISBN 0-8027-7400-8 (paper)

Text design by Laurie McBarnette

Printed in Hong Kong

2 4 6 8 10 9 7 5 3 1

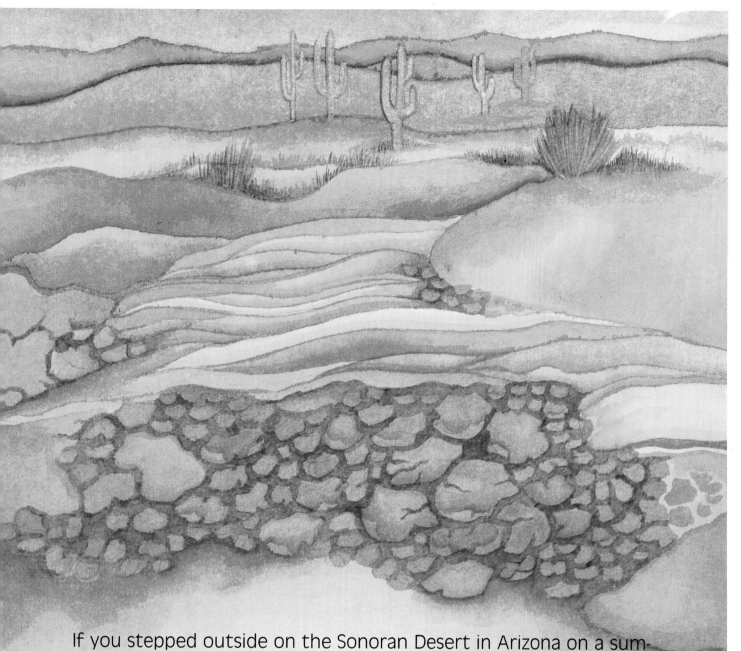

If you stepped outside on the Sonoran Desert in Arizona on a summer day, the first thing you would notice is the heat. The hot air hits you in the face like opening an oven door. Temperatures in the summer can go as high as 130 degrees. But in spite of the heat, you don't notice that you're sweating. That's because the air is so dry here that perspiration instantly evaporates, leaving behind a gritty film of white salt on your skin. A grown man could lose a quart of liquid from his body in an hour. A day without water in this blazing sun could cause death.

It's dryness that makes a desert. There are many deserts around the world. Some deserts, like the sandy Sahara, seem quite lifeless. Others, like the Sonoran Desert, have so many plants they are called "green" deserts. But they all have one thing in common. If you could catch rain as it falls on any desert for a year, you would not fill a coffee can. Deserts are places where rainfall is less than ten inches per year. Very little rain means very little water in the ground. And all living things need water to live. Is there something special about the plants, animals, and people of a desert like the Sonoran? You bet!

There are three ways plants survive with very little water. The first is to be able to go into a kind of "sleep," or *dormancy*. The creosote bush is sometimes called a "greasewood" tree because its leaves are coated with a thick wax that keeps water from evaporating from the leaves. Even so, water can be lost here, so the leaves drop off during a long dry spell. As the months of dryness go on, the creosote bush loses its branches and the bush looks brown and dead. But when it rains, it amazingly springs back to life, growing new branches and leaves in a few weeks.

The second way plants survive dryness is to grow and make new seeds when there is water. The part of a plant that makes seeds is the flower. Seeds may have to wait years where they drop, for a rare fall rain which makes them come to life again. A few days after such a rain, the seeds start to sprout. In the spring different kinds of flowers carpet the desert. People rush to see a spectacular desert bloom because it only happens about every ten years or so.

A third way plants live through dry periods is to store water after a rain. There are many different kinds of plants that store water, but the most famous is the cactus. The water is stored in the cacti's stems, some of which work like accordions. After a rainfall the stem expands with water. During a dry spell, the zigzag shape lets the cactus shrink without wilting.

Cacti have a large circle of shallow roots to absorb water. When it rains, they quickly grow tiny extra roots to take up as much rainwater as possible before it runs off the hard, sandy soil and evaporates.

The juicy stems of cacti can be a source of water for thirsty animals, birds, and people. But nature protects the cacti. Some cacti have sap that is thick and poisonous or that tastes terrible. Most cacti grow sharp spines or thorns for protection, but at times the spines aren't enough. Some cattle will eat cactus, spines and all, if they get hungry enough. And spines don't bother the javelinas (have-a-LEEN-a), the wild, piglike animals whose favorite food is the prickly-pear cactus.

One kind of spiny cactus is called "jumping cholla" (CHOY-ah). Its spines will stick to you so easily that people say they jump at you. Cowboys wear leather chaps to protect their legs from cactus thorns. Even so, the tiny cholla spines get into their skin. Cowboys tell of getting spines in a leg or arm, which work their way out someplace else, like their shoulders, a few months later. Still, the cowboys have learned to get to the juicy flesh of the jumping cholla by burning off the spines. Then the stem can be sliced open and the soft, green, almost sweet pulp can be scooped out.

Cactus thorns at one time have been used by desert Indians as fish hooks, sewing needles, and needles for making tattoos on the skin.

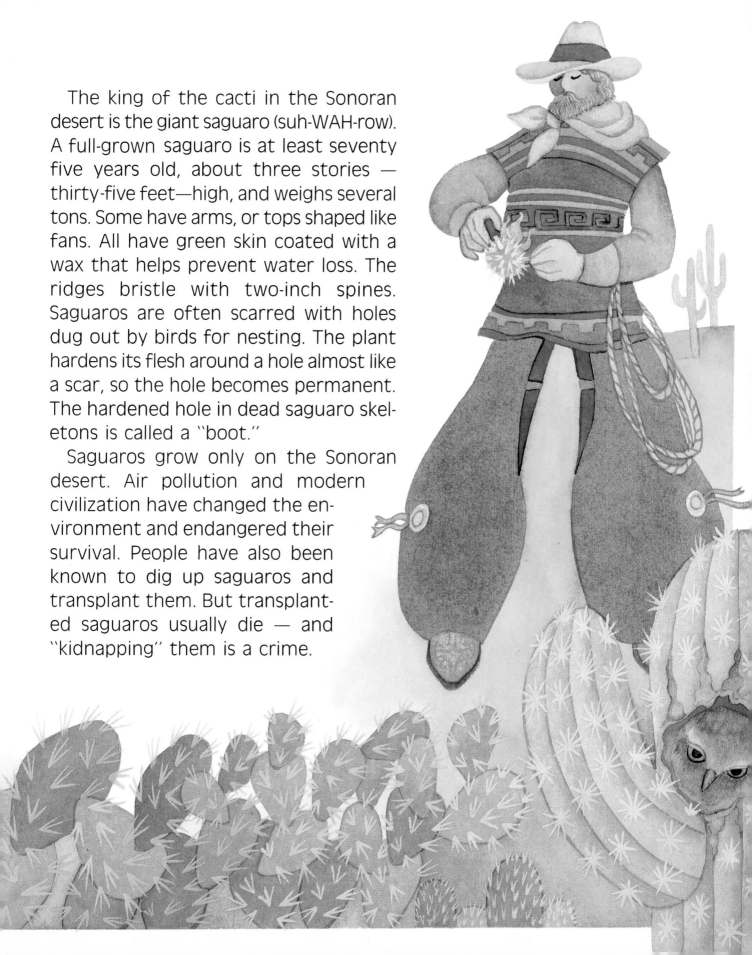

The king of the cacti in the Sonoran desert is the giant saguaro (suh-WAH-row). A full-grown saguaro is at least seventy five years old, about three stories — thirty-five feet—high, and weighs several tons. Some have arms, or tops shaped like fans. All have green skin coated with a wax that helps prevent water loss. The ridges bristle with two-inch spines. Saguaros are often scarred with holes dug out by birds for nesting. The plant hardens its flesh around a hole almost like a scar, so the hole becomes permanent. The hardened hole in dead saguaro skeletons is called a "boot."

Saguaros grow only on the Sonoran desert. Air pollution and modern civilization have changed the environment and endangered their survival. People have also been known to dig up saguaros and transplant them. But transplanted saguaros usually die — and "kidnapping" them is a crime.

In May, the tops of full-grown saguaros bloom. It's not easy to get a look at the beautiful, creamy white, trumpet-shaped flowers. They open only at night—out of the heat of the sun—and last only about eighteen hours. This is just enough time for the saguaro's seeds to be pollinated by birds and bats that sip the flowers' nectar. Pollination makes the fruit around the seeds develop.

Saguaro fruit are the size of plums and are enclosed in greenish husks. Inside is a bright red pulp filled with more than two thousand tiny seeds. The fruit tastes like a raspberry flavored fig.

Tohono O'Odham (Toe-HOE-no Oh-oh-DOM) Indians pick the fruit before it drops using long poles made from the ribs of the woody skeletons of dead saguaros. Each cactus produces several hundred fruit. The Indians cook the fruit and strain out the seeds to make syrup, candy, and jelly for the rest of the year.

Cactus spines aren't the only things that can stick you on the desert. There are insects, spiders, lizards, and snakes. Some have venomous stings and bites. And yes, they can harm you if you don't watch out!

The scorpion's tail is a stinging machine. Scorpions hunt at night for insects, spiders, and tiny baby mice. They hold their victim in their front pincers and sting it until it is paralyzed. A scorpion sting is painful but it is not likely to kill anyone.

The black widow spider kills its prey with a venomous bite. The female is famous for her treatment of her mate. After a male spider wanders into the web of the female and mates with her, she eats him. This provides special nourishment for the eggs, which develop in her body before they are laid. In nature, even a parent can be sacrificed in the interest of the next generation. The most important thing is for the species to survive.

The tarantula is one of the largest spiders in the world. Adults can grow up to be six inches long. They are covered with hair and have fangs to capture the animals they eat. They also have tiny hairs on the top rear of their abdomens that contain venom. When it is threatened, the tarantula protects itself by using its hind legs to brush the hairs towards its enemy. These hairs cause itching and sores on people.

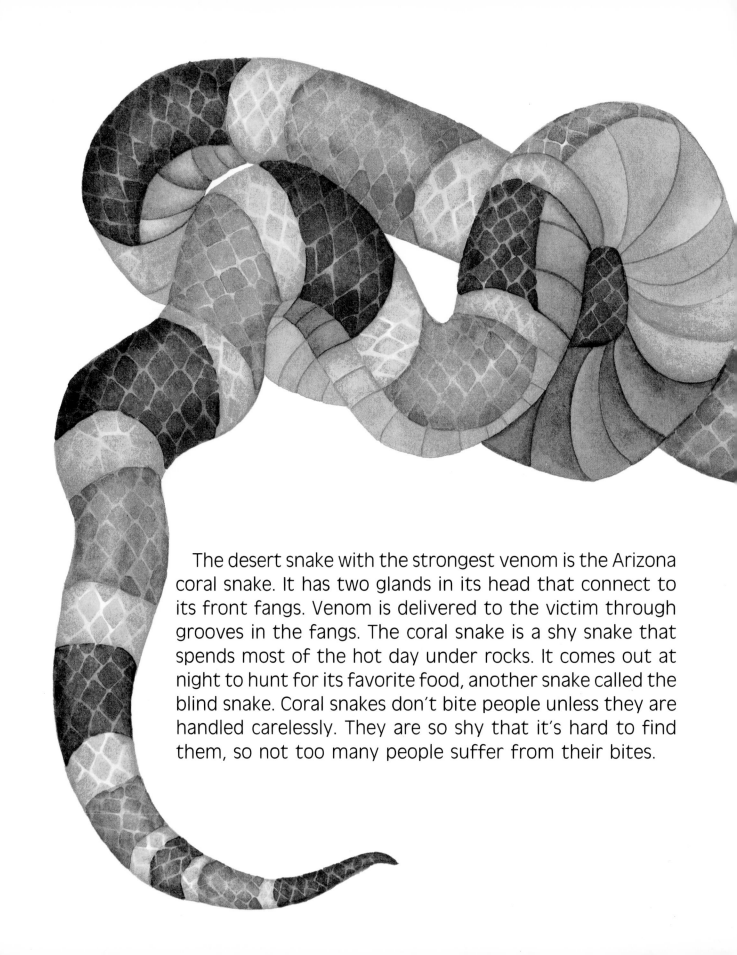

The desert snake with the strongest venom is the Arizona coral snake. It has two glands in its head that connect to its front fangs. Venom is delivered to the victim through grooves in the fangs. The coral snake is a shy snake that spends most of the hot day under rocks. It comes out at night to hunt for its favorite food, another snake called the blind snake. Coral snakes don't bite people unless they are handled carelessly. They are so shy that it's hard to find them, so not too many people suffer from their bites.

A coral snake is easy to recognize. It has wide bands of red and black that are separated by narrower rings of pale yellow. There are other desert snakes that look like the deadly coral snake. Being a ``copycat'' provides protection, because snake-eating birds and animals are fooled and stay away. But the copycats are not perfect copies. They have black bands on either side of the yellow, and the yellow bands are never next to the red as they are on the real thing. As they say in the desert: ``Red on yellow can kill a fellow; red on black's no threat to Jack.''

The most dangerous snakes in the desert are the eleven different kinds of rattlesnakes. Rattlesnakes are named for the sound they make when they shake their tails. The end of the rattlesnake's tail has about eight loosely connected sections. When a rattlesnake is threatened, it shakes its tail, making a whirring sound that warns its enemies it's about to strike. But when a rattlesnake hunts, it keeps very quiet.

The two most famous rattlesnakes of the Sonoran desert are the sidewinder and the diamondback. They are not as venomous as coral snakes, but they are not as shy, either. The sidewinder is known for its peculiar sidewise movement over the sandy soil. The diamondback is the largest rattlesnake and can be more than six feet long.

Rattlesnakes use their venomous bite to kill small animals like the kangaroo rat and birds. They have very poor eyesight, so how do they know when to strike with their deadly fangs? With the help of two amazing "pits" under the eye on either side of their head. The pits detect a prey by the heat it gives off. They are so sensitive that they can sense a difference in the surrounding temperature of only one degree, telling the snake exactly where its prey is located. After biting an animal, the snake waits for the venom to paralyze it. Sometimes the wounded animal wanders away before it dies. Then the snake finds it by flicking its forked tongue in and out. The tongue is connected to the Jacobson's organ in the mouth which detects the fallen prey by its smell. The snake eats by stretching its mouth around its prey and seems to creep around its food.

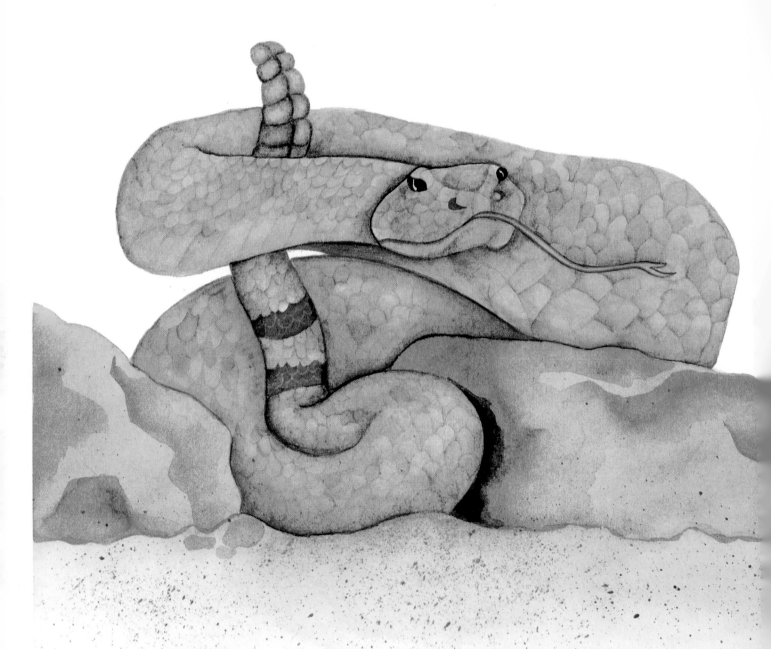

The rattlesnake's worst enemy is the roadrunner, a sixteen-inch-high, long-legged and flightless bird. The roadrunner holds the record as the fastest running bird on the North American continent. It can run twenty-six miles per hour and jump up to ten feet in the air. It kills a rattlesnake by kicking and pecking at it. The rattlesnake, of course, tries to strike back with its fangs. But the roadrunner is too quick, and can usually get out of the way. Roadrunners eat snakes and small lizards.

There is only one venomous lizard in the desert. It's called the Gila (HE-la) monster. The Gila's favorite food is quail eggs, but it will also eat young rabbits and squirrels. You can tell how well-fed a Gila monster is by how fat its tail is. Gila monsters are the largest lizards in the desert and can be between one and two feet long. Gila monsters are slow to bite, but once they have bitten they hang on. This gives the venom a chance to run down the grooves of their teeth into the wound. Most bites come from careless handling of the lizard by people who don't have proper respect for its dangers.

The desert has its share of bats, rabbits, squirrels, and mice. Most of these small mammals are active at night when it is cooler. The larger mammals include the javelinas and mule deer, known for their large ears. Some of the desert animals have been hunted so much that they are protected from hunters by law. Jaguars, bighorn sheep, and prong-horns (antelopes) are on the list of protected species.

There are two very unusual small desert mammals. The kangaroo rat is especially suited to the dry desert because it never needs to drink water. Its body is able to get the water it needs from seeds, the only food it eats.

The packrat is busy all night at its two favorite activities: eating seeds and building its nest. It is an amazing architect. The foundation of a packrat nest is made with pieces of the jumping cholla cactus, whose bristling spines act as protection from invaders. They don't seem to bother the tiny packrat, who grabs one long spine to drag a piece of the cactus to its nest. The packrat nest may be located in a prickly pear patch or in a cave. The nest can be huge, sometimes six feet across and three feet high, weighing more than a ton, because the packrat is never finished building. It seems to need to keep carrying things to its nest, adding all kinds of objects: twigs, feathers, string, almost anything it can carry off. It especially likes shiny objects. People have lost bullets, jewelry, and even gold nuggets to a packrat who left behind some dried bones or mushrooms in their place. It's not that the packrat was making a trade, though. It just dropped what it was carrying in favor of an object it liked better.

People live on the desert, too. It is warm and the air is clear and dry. But people have to have water just like the plants and animals. Water even makes it possible to farm the desert. About 300 B.C., the Hohokam Indians settled by the Salt River which runs through the Sonoran Desert. It's no surprise that they were corn farmers. Corn was developed from a kind of grass by the Indians. As long as there is a source of water, it grows easily almost anywhere. In addition to corn, though, the Hohokams grew vegetables and cotton. They made pots of clay from desert soil and baskets from desert grasses.

As the Hohokam community grew, it became harder and harder to carry water from the river for its crops. So the Hohokams dug canals from the river to their fields. In all, they dug over two hundred miles of canals, using hoes made of stone. An incredible task!

The Hohokams lived by the Salt River for 1600 years. Then they left—and no one knows why. Their name has come to mean "the people who went away." We know about them because today's archeologists have uncovered and studied the ruins of their villages and the remains of their canals, which had slowly filled up with soft dirt.

Two hundred years after the Hohokams left, other people began discovering the Salt River Valley. The Spanish in Mexico knew about it. Miners passed through it on their way to silver and gold mines. In the nineteenth century pioneers passed through on their way to California. But not many people settled there. It looked dry and dusty.

   In the late 1860s a man named Jack Swilling noticed the remains of the Hohokam canals. He figured that people would settle in the valley if they could water their crops, so he started the Swilling Ditch Company to redig the canals and to irrigate the valley. The town of Phoenix was built on the remains of the old Hohokam settlement. It got its name from an old Egyptian story about a bird that was destroyed in a fire but rose from its ashes to live again.

The irrigation canals in the Salt River Valley changed it into green farmland. People further west needed food, and it was too expensive to bring it from the East. Besides, the climate was good and the land was free to people who would build homes there. Water for home use could come from ground water in wells and from the irrigation canals.

Settlers had to deal with the hot summers and they used water to help. Evaporating water cools things. People sprinkled the dirt floors of their thick-walled adobe houses with water. As the water evaporated the air cooled off. They kept their food in "desert refrigerators," which were simply boxes covered with a coarse cloth. A can on top dripped water over the cloth. As the water evaporated the air inside the box was cooled.

If Phoenix was to grow and become a city, there had to be a more certain water supply. Even the irrigation ditches didn't help when there was a drought. There was a major water source to be had from melting snow in the mountains—but they were eighty miles away. The only way to collect this water would be to build a dam and create a lake. A daring and expensive idea! It took several years for the federal government to agree to lend the money for the project. It took another two years for the almost five thousand landowners in the Salt River Valley to agree to share both the water and the cost of the loan. Then a road eighty miles long had to be built to the dam site through mountains and canyons. Heavy machinery was hauled up by mules. A concrete plant was built close to the dam site. Little by little, each difficulty was overcome.

The Roosevelt Dam was dedicated by President Theodore Roosevelt himself in the spring of 1911. It created the first and largest of six reservoirs built to supply water to the city of Phoenix and the Salt River Valley. Besides storing water, the dams of the Salt River Project help produce electricity. Even better, this was the beginning of a reliable water supply, making desert living quite comfortable. Residents of Phoenix now have as much water as people who live in an area that gets twenty inches of rain a year.

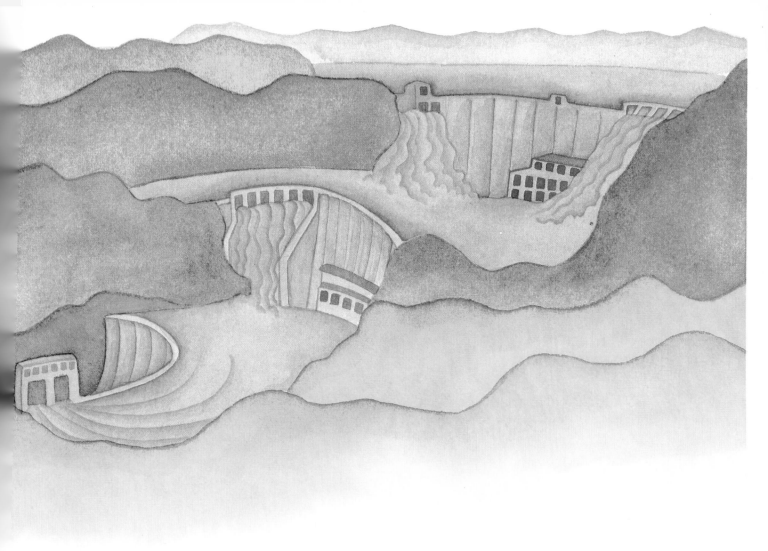

People who live in the Salt River Valley have plenty of water for bathing, cooking, and laundry. They can even water their lawns and wash their cars. Some lawns are watered by flooding them every so often. The canal system based on the old Hohokam canals brings water to the yard. Valves are opened, and two to five inches of water covers the lawn and sinks into the ground. This conserves water that would be lost to evaporation if a sprinkler system were used.

In spite of the seemingly plentiful water supply, however, residents are aware that water must be conserved. People pay for the water they use. Some people don't even bother with lawns. Instead, they landscape their yards with the water-efficient plants of the desert.

Arizonans boast that they have 360 days of sunshine a year and temperatures ranging between 44 and 106 degrees. There are two rainy periods. In the spring, torrential monsoon rains bring most of the rain for the year, about two and a half inches. In the winter there are a few days of fine drizzle—and that's all. Fourteen different Indian tribes live on or near the Sonoran desert. They are known for their baskets and for their beautifully decorated pots and their silver and turquoise jewelry. The desert landscape inspires many artists. Visitors come to enjoy all the desert has to offer. They imagine living here. Can you?